INEVITABLE BALANCE

INEVITABLE BALANCE

Understanding Why "What Goes Around Comes Around"—A Monograph

J. Bartholomew Walker

Quadrakoff Publications Group, LLC
Wilmington, Delaware
USA

Copyright ©2020, 2017 Quadrakoff Publications Group, LLC All rights reserved.

Except as noted, All NASB scriptures taken from The New American Standard Bible® Copyright © 1960, 1962, 1963, 1968, 1971, 1972, 1973, 1975, 1977, 1995 by the Lockman Foundation, LaHabra, CA.

Special thanks to the Lockman Foundation for the finest Bible version available; as well as for their permission to use the same. All Scripture passages taken from The Holy Bible, King James Version, are as noted.

ISBN: 978-1-948219-15-0

All rights reserved. No part of this publication may be reproduced, stored in a retrieval system or transmitted, in any form, or by any means, electronic, mechanical, recorded, photocopied, or otherwise, without the prior written permission of both the copyright owner and the above publisher of this book, except by a reviewer who may quote brief passages in a review.

The scanning, uploading, and distribution of this book via the Internet or via any other means without the permission of the publisher is illegal and punishable by law. Please purchase only authorized electronic editions and do not participate in or encourage electronic piracy of copyrightable materials. Your support of the author's rights is appreciated.

Any and all characters appearing that are not in any of the versions of the Bible are fictional. Any resemblance to any living person is strictly coincidental. Some portions of this Monograph can also be found in "*MeekRaker Beginnings…*"

Cover art courtesy of NASA.

Printed in the United States of America.

Man sometimes sees one when there are two; and sometimes sees two when there is but one. The first error is seen with perception of that which is alive. The second occurs when evaluating man's actions. That which is referred to as karma, *is not a separate entity; but rather is inextricably contained in the original action—whether admitted or not.*

INEVITABLE BALANCE

What is *balance*?

If used as a noun, this represents some type of device utilized for balancing. Of course using a word in its definition helps little. But if it can be so stipulated that balance is derived from the Latin *bi*, meaning two; and the Latin *lanx*, meaning "dish or plate;"[1] then an image of the "scales" such as those representing the "scales of justice" comes to mind.

But much more importantly, balance as a noun can also represent a state of *equilibrium*.

If used as a verb, this then represents the act of achieving the second meaning of the noun—equilibrium. So here when one expends effort in order to *balance* something; the desired result is *balance*.

Kinetic energy is the energy that "a thing" has because it is in *motion*. Depending upon one's perspective, it can be said that a thing in motion is in actuality in the act of *attaining balance*. Or it could also be said that a thing in motion *is* in balance. Hit a baseball with a bat, and the ball then has kinetic energy from the force imparted to it by the bat. The ball will travel until other forces act upon it and bring it to a stop—most particularly gravity and wind resistance. [However due to the *inertia* of the ball, or any thing "in motion," the same will remain in motion until acted upon by another force, such as said gravity and wind resistance.] Thus this motion or kinetic energy could also be considered as a form of balance, but generally not in the material world. Even the planets are believed to be slowing down, however gradually.

Potential energy is energy that is *stored*. Here; again depending upon perspective; either a *balanced* or an *unbalanced* situation is present, and will remain present, unless and until the potential energy is released. A rock perched on the very edge of a cliff has potential energy, representing both a balance and an imbalance. Should the vibrations from a thunderstorm be sufficient to dislodge this perched rock, this potential energy then becomes kinetic energy as the rock is then in motion. Once the rock comes to a rest, that particular potential energy no longer exists. However, unless and until the rock is dislodged laterally by some force, it is also in a sense balanced.

Potential energy can be converted to kinetic energy, and kinetic energy can result in potential energy. Just ask the child who threw the ball that ended up "stuck" on the roof. If he could just dislodge it with a stick, it would fall to the ground. Or in the case of a pendulum; when moving; the pendulum has kinetic energy; and then potential energy when it stops, just before changing direction. Older watches require "winding," which is introducing kinetic energy, which produces potential energy in the spring. This potential energy is then released slowly as kinetic energy, moving the hands of the watch, until insufficient potential energy remains in the spring.

This kinetic-potential-kinetic conversion process is a very important concept, as along with free will; represent what could very well be considered as the "key" or the "keys," to, or of, the universe—assuming any such "keys" exist.

There are many forms of *material* potential energy, even that which is contained in the atoms that undergo fission or fusion in a nuclear reaction. Batteries and electric power represent material potential energy.

There is also *immaterial* potential energy. If this sounds a bit insane, then purposely insult, (stimulus), someone until they respond, (response). As these insults continue, there is immaterial potential energy being "created" and "stored" in the mind of the recipient of the insults. This immaterial potential energy exists until released, and is largely; although not necessarily exclusively; released as *material* kinetic energy, if and when there is a response.

Materially; there can be both internal as well as external responses to the insults, in attempts to achieve some degree of balance. The material *externals* are somewhat easy to detect—often verbal or physical. Increase in heart rate, respiration, and blood pressure can be considered as material *internal* responses.

Assuming the response is verbal; immaterial potential energy will subsequently then build in the *recipient* (source of original stimulus) of this response. And even when the response is physical; (better duck); the same holds true. And back and forth this can go until some degree and some type of balance is achieved.

It is also quite possible that this immaterial potential energy might not be released at that time. "Revenge is a dish best served cold," being a prime example.

Immaterial potential energy is by no means limited to the above. Terms such as "drive," "passion," and "determination;" all represent examples of immaterial potential energy, and there are many more. "I'm going to give him a piece of my mind;" or "I want satisfaction;" or "Who does she think she is?;" each represents evidence of immaterial potential energy. These potential energies will generally either become material kinetic energy, or will "dissipate" over time, causing changes elsewhere. Said "dissipation" can often result in health issues. This is one main reason why forgiveness is important. Forgiveness is not necessarily for the benefit of the perpetrator; as the same might not know, care, or even *believe* that there is anything requiring forgiveness. Forgiveness helps channel this immaterial potential energy elsewhere, often to the benefit of the "forgiver."

How much *immaterial* potential energy is there present in the above "insult" scenario? There are infinite possibilities of answers. The actual immaterial potential energy "created," is the result of many subjective and objective factors; but what is always the case, is that it is a "difference of potential."

The same is true materially with the flow of electricity. A charged 12V battery has the voltage or "difference of potential" of 12V, and electrons (I) will flow according to the resistance of the load (R) in this DC (direct current) circuit. A completely discharged battery essentially has a difference of potential of zero, and nothing will flow; unless and until the battery is "charged."

In fact, the use of the word *charge* itself in many contexts relates either to the imposition of an imbalance; or sometimes can refer to the actions undertaken to balance an existing imbalance.

The discharged or "dead" battery is a balanced phenomenon. It contains little or no potential energy, or difference of potential. The act of *charging* a discharged battery causes an imbalance, by providing a difference of potential between the two contacts. It is then the subsequent *balancing* of this imbalance; that is by design the purpose of the battery. The imbalance of a charged battery represents stored or potential energy, for the very purpose of discharging this energy, until the battery again becomes balanced or discharged.

A *criminal* charge causes an imbalance that will be balanced by some type of adjudication. This imbalance can remain for some period of time. There is a prosecutor that generally initiates this imbalance.

In fact the very word prosecutor itself alludes to this. The prefix "pro," generally means *before*; and the "secutor," appears to be related to *sequence* or what follows.

The prosecutor expends energy to create this imbalance *before* whatever *follows*; e.g; punishment. Thus the very term *prosecutor* indicates *causing* an imbalance. Why does the prosecutor cause this imbalance? This is normally done, because the accused is believed to have previously caused an imbalance to another by his or her actions, or lack thereof. The prosecutor creates imbalances, in order to balance a previous imbalance or imbalances.

Juries are *charged* by the judge, by instructing them as to the law; and then after conclusion of the matter or mistrial are *discharged*. In a sense, the obligation for balancing the imbalance caused by the prosecutor, is transferred to the jury after the presentation of all facts. The jury's imbalance or burden is the determination of guilt or lack of guilt; (not guilty as opposed to *innocent*); based upon facts as presented and the law.

Whatever it is that is determined, this then transfers the imbalance back to the judge for sentencing and then to "corrections" if guilty; or transferred back to the prosecutor if unable to reach a verdict, or released if acquitted.

The imbalance of a "hung jury," is then placed upon the prosecutor with regard to a retrial; or in the case of an acquittal, this imbalance is partially balanced by some degree of diminution of the reputation of the prosecutor.

One who is *in charge*, has the responsibility, (imbalance), of managing something; e.g.; "Who is in charge here?;" or "the boss is charged with . . ." Or; when one is placed *in the charge* of another, said other has an imbalance placed upon him or her by being given the responsibility for another person.

"Charge" can also be the balance for the imbalance created by purchase or consumption of goods or services, often used in lieu of "price" or "cost." From the *consumer's* standpoint, monies due on a "charge account" represent an imbalance, which must be balanced. From the *creditor's* standpoint, a charge account is unbalanced when there are no monies due; as this is the business they are in. Thus when there are monies due, this is "carrying a balance;" and when no monies are due, there is "no balance."

An alternative explanation being, that "carry" here means a burden that must be met. Thus here "carrying a balance" represents an imbalanced state to the borrower.

As an aside, it is not difficult to attribute "death measurement" as a literal definition to the word "mortgage." Creditors prefer to receive interest payments for the entire remaining life of the borrower, so they then tailor the loan to the borrower's life expectancy.

J. Bartholomew Walker

Immaterial Kinetic Energy

Thus far; *material* potential energy, and *material* kinetic energy were addressed, along with a brief mention of *immaterial potential* energy. There is something else which was deliberately left "un-addressed" until now. The same being, whether or not there exists the phenomenon of *immaterial kinetic* energy?

In order to understand the answer to this, a closer examination of immaterial *potential* energy is helpful.

In an unrealistic "all other things being equal" sense, an immaterial *potential* energy or difference of potential *increase*, represents the *difference* between the existing level of "balance" *prior* to the introduction of the new stimulus; and the magnitude of the *total* imbalance, including that which was caused by said new stimulus.

With respect to the "insult" scenario; since no one is completely "balanced," *relative* degrees of imbalance must be utilized.

It is true that the level of any prior imbalance can disproportionately affect the increase in imbalance caused by a new stimulus; but that is "on the recipient." Meaning; that if it is true that "he's just crabby," or "she's just upset about something else;" disproportional increases in immaterial potential energy will exist, but not necessarily having been solely caused by that stimulus.

This Δ or change, (here increase), in *imbalance* from that level which existed prior to the new stimulus; represents the immaterial potential energy *increase* for that particular new stimulus. Thus the increase in "difference of potential," is this Δ for that particular new stimulus.

$$IPE_T = IPE_O + IPE_S$$

or

$$IPE_S = IPE_T - IPE_O$$

Here the total immaterial potential energy, is equal to the *original* immaterial potential energy, (IPE_O); plus the additional imbalance created by the *new* stimulus, (IPE_S).

Or; the increase in immaterial potential energy due to the stimulus, (IPE_S); is equal to the "post stimulus" total, (IPE_T), minus what was originally present prior to the new stimulus, (IPE_O).

Just as there are virtually unlimited possibilities for this Δ, or increase in immaterial potential energy because of differences in the perceptions of people and situations; the same can be said for that which then becomes the *kinetic* energy (response).

Thus the ultimate *balancing* of the increase in immaterial *potential* energy, is also subject to these same possibilities. What can and should be said however; is that the sane *objective* of any response should be *justice*, with the *goal* being *balance*.

When there is an obviously disproportionally large kinetic response to a given stimulus; this is often referred to as "petty." Meaning; that the *kinetic* response to a stimulus was much greater that that which would be considered as reasonable. When this kinetic response is disproportionately high, this is likely due to, (the balancing of), a disproportionately large immaterial *potential* energy change. The question is why?

If a given stimulus is considered as s, and the response is considered r; it must be asked as to why there can be such a variety of possible *quantities* and *qualities* for r, with each being a response to the very same stimulus, or the same given s?

Stated a bit differently, $A \times B = C$; here with A representing the *stimulus*, B representing the person or *recipient*, and C representing the *reaction* of the recipient.

In a room full of people, all who are receiving precisely the same stimulus; both the *quantity* and *qualitiy* of C will be different for each person receiving this same stimulus. Therefore since A is a constant, the plethora of different responses cannot be a function of A. Thus any variations in C; must then necessarily be the result of variations in B; or the individual recipient.

The answer is that which is universally so; and yet produces the confusion. The same being; that *all* human beings act from the standpoint of *reality*—as there is no other choice. This is stated with the understanding that the term "all" is quite inclusive. How can this be so?

This answer lies in the definition of *reality*. *Reality* is what is *perceived* or *believed* to be so. This is in contradistinction to *actuality*, which is what (actually) *is* so.

That which is a mirage; but is not known to be a mirage; represents a *reality* of water, with an *actuality* of "not water;" e.g.; sand. This *reality* of water will be acted upon by traveling a great distance; only to then ultimately find that the previous reality, and the actuality, are quite different; producing a new *reality* for this very same actuality.

The seemingly disproportional response by the "petty" person, is considered as such; because of the different *realities* produced by the same stimulus, (an *actuality*). Even words that are considered as innocuous by most; can cause massive increases in immaterial potential energy in those, who for whatever reason(s), are sensitive to these terms.

And obviously this increase in this immaterial potential energy, is likely to produce a much larger, (kinetic), response. The observers of the "petty" person, know not of the reality produced in others; but know only of that which is produced in themselves, and thus do not understand this reaction.

Here it is not so much the *actuality* that is responsible, but rather that the *reality*, as is the case with the mirage, is disproportionately altered; but here likely because of some past experiences.

This forms the basis for "politically correct" speech. Some person or group of persons makes a determination as to what their particular sensitivity is to be; and then requires all others to then use terminology that is "sensitive" to these purported "sensitivities."

Surely there are *legitimate* sensitivities to certain words or phrases, as a result of past experiences; and the same, if known, should be respected. However these legitimate sensitivities are based upon actualities, and thus do not fall into the category of that which is generally known as "politically correct."

Even seemingly simple actualities are so startlingly complex, that no reality can ever be equal to an actuality. Actuality represents the set, and reality, (if and when accurate), represents merely a subset or subsets. What is vital; is that it is always the case that the subset of *reality,* however small a fraction of the actuality; is always contained within the larger set of *actuality*.

For a material example: The *actuality* of electricity; is generally only perceived by its effects. One does not generally perceive the electrons flowing, or the expanding and contracting fields surrounding the house wiring; yet each is part of the actuality. And the "actual actuality" is that almost all matter is atomic or molecular; and even the atoms, including the atoms comprising molecules, have subsets of "particles."

Thus physicists, chemists, and consumers have different *realities* of the *actuality* known as electricity. And although none represent 100% reality of said actuality; all that is truly "known," (tautology?), represents merely a *subset* of the actuality.

When the *reality* is not part of, or a subset of, the actuality; this then represents a *false* reality. But even those who believe there are "pink elephants" in the room, are nevertheless acting from the *reality* of the existence of said elephants; despite the fact that there is no such actuality.

But once again: "Is there any such thing as *immaterial* kinetic energy; and if so, what does that even mean?"

Probably the best known example of *immaterial* kinetic energy, is that which is often described as the "Big Bang;" or perhaps better stated, that which *caused* the "Big Bang."

Simply put, the "Big Bang" is the *event* of the creation of the universe. The *universe* in this usage refers to the creation of time, space, and matter. Another way to describe the *universe*; would be to call it the *material* or the *natural* realm. So this "Big Bang" event can be called either the *creation* of the *universe*; or the creation of the *material* realm, or the creation of the *natural* realm.

It is inarguable that prior to the creation of matter, there was not matter. Therefore; there could have existed neither *material* potential energy, nor *material* kinetic energy, prior to the creation of the material.

And since the use of material and immaterial to describe two realms is a *binary*—there is either matter contained in a given "realm," or there is not; this leaves *immaterial* potential energy and *immaterial* kinetic energy as the only possible causes for the creation of the universe.

And since potential energy represents only *potential*; but kinetic energy represents *action*, (something's happening); by Hobson's choice, the *cause* of said "Big Bang" had to have been *immaterial* kinetic energy.

This is precisely why no *material cause* can ever, or will ever, be found for the *effect* known as the universe, or the material realm.

Simply put; one cannot find a *cause* for a given phenomenon contained within that same phenomenon, until said, (second), phenomenon exists.

If there were a *material cause* for the effect known as the universe or the material realm; it would had to have emanated from said realm prior to this very realm's existence, Meaning; that said cause would had to have existed in a phenomenon, *prior* to the creation; i.e.; the bringing into existence of; this very same phenomenon.

At the time of the "Big Bang," there was no material realm from which the cause for the creation of the material realm could have emanated.

It must also be asked, if it is possible to have either material or immaterial *kinetic* energy, without having said energy first existing in the *potential* form? Can there be any "action," without first having the *potential* for this action?

Genesis 1:1 tells us:

"In the beginning God created the heaven(s) and the earth."[2]

It must be remembered that the word here translated as "created," is in fact the Hebrew word bârâ; meaning to bring into existence from *nothing* or "no thing." This is in contradistinction to the Hebrew word yâtsar, generally translated as *formed*; which of course then requires *something* material from which to yâtsar or form.

The Bible tells us that this, (yâtsar), was the case with Adam, as Adam was not brought into existence via bârâ; but rather was *formed* from 'âphâr, generally translated as "dust."

It is from this pandemic misunderstanding of the *process*, that the purported conflict between the scientific and Scriptural age of the earth arises—Adam was *formed*, and thus not one of the original *created* hosts. [A much greater detailed analysis of this can be found in "*MeekRaker Beginnings...*"]

Here in Genesis 1:1 we are told about the *creation* of the universe, or the material realm. If one could have been an observer to the events described in Genesis 1:1, one would have witnessed what is generally scientifically referred to as the "Big Bang."

Some "Bible versions" (note these are not called translations), "translate" "heaven" in the singular. This translation presents a similar problem, because God could not have resided in a yet to be created realm prior to the time when He created said realm.

The use of the term "heaven" in the *singular*, generally refers to the *immaterial* realm where God resides; e.g.; the "heaven" in "Who art in heaven." This refers to the *immaterial* realm.

The use of the *plural* of heaven, "heavens;" generally refers to the space between the celestial bodies, and thus is contained in the *material* realm.

From man's perspective in the *material* realm, where there *is* time, space, and matter; there had to be a *cause* for the creation of the heavens and the earth, ("Big Bang"); which *preceded* this creative event.

From the perspective of the *immaterial* realm, from where, ("whence"), this cause necessarily must have emanated; the same realm where there is no time, space, or matter; any type of *sequencing* is extremely difficult, if not impossible, to comprehend.

Nevertheless; "This is where we are," ("are at").

Most major religions consider God to be *omnipotent*. This could be defined as "all potent;" or complete or unlimited *potential*; the key words here being *potent* or *potential*.

Once again, *all* is a rather inclusive term, leaving little room for debate. Omnipotent refers to one *characteristic* of God. If this characteristic itself is examined, it could be described as "omni-potential," or "all potentials."

But what is or are "all potentials?" That is the set containing all things that are possible. The "all potentials" set, does not include that which is not possible.

J. Bartholomew Walker

Matthew 19:26 tells us:

*"But Jesus beheld them, and said unto them,
with men this is impossible,
but with God all things are possible."*[3]

If this passage is read as actually written in the KJV, rather than as it is usually interpreted; a qualifier is unmistakably noted. Jesus did not say "all is possible," but rather that "all *things* are possible." (italics supplied)

Meaning that if it is a thing, it is possible; but if it is not a thing, then "it" does not fall into the category of "possible"—at least with respect to this particular passage.

What are "things?" The actual Greek word in this passage translated as "things," could not be found anywhere in the original Strong's.

But if it is so stipulated that "things" means the set of that, (Male/Female/Neuter), which exists or could exist; then the passage tell us that: "All that exists or could exist are possible;" but appears here with a qualifier. Without the qualifier, the statement "All that exists or could exist is/are possible;" would otherwise qualify as merely a tautology, with little or no educational value.

This qualifier is significant, but becomes especially significant if examined in context. *"With men this is impossible,*" "*but with God;*" "All that exists or could exist are possible;" represents two conditions.

Firstly, that this seems to refer not only to what already exists, but what might exist "*are possible*," in the future.

Secondly, with the contextual use of "*with;*" it is more than arguable that contextually this refers to men acting "*with*" God, rather man acting alone, ("*with men this is impossible*").

Neither does this seem to refer to God acting alone, and furthermore; that this, (men acting with God), is the very purpose for the statement.

What things are *not* possible even with God? God cannot act against His own *will*. Whatever He chooses; *is* His will.

God cannot arbitrarily change His laws for one entity, while maintaining them for another. Two must remain two, and not be two when one person writes a check; but then be fifteen when this same person deposits another's check in the same amount of two— else the universe might cease to exist.

God must act according to His laws; else he would simultaneously be acting consistent with two different and contradictory, and possibly even mutually exclusive, wills.

Since God has all potentials, how do we know what all these potentials are? The answer is that we don't, and likely could not understand them if we did.

But what *can* be done; is to examine what He has done, and thereby derive what some of these potentials are or were. [*Were* rather than *are* must be included here, as it is unclear that once the immaterial *potential* energy for "a thing" is converted into immaterial *kinetic* energy; whether said *potential* continues to exist in the immaterial realm. This could help explain why Adam was *formed* from matter, and not *created* from nothing, as was the case with the original created hosts.]

Genesis 1:1 tells us what happened, describing the *effects* of this immaterial kinetic energy. Later in Genesis, with the *"And God said let..., and there was;"* again shows us God putting this immaterial potential energy into action.

This is known because prior to the *result*, or the *"and there was;"* clearly there was not. The "let" is the point of conversion of the immaterial *potential* into the immaterial *kinetic*, and we are told the result. This is the expression of free will, and the resultant balance.

As already stated, man is by design an entity capable of *immaterial* potential energy; which in man generally is balanced by or results in *material* kinetic energy.

The question now, is whether man is capable of balancing this immaterial *potential* energy with immaterial *kinetic* energy in any significant way; instead of merely achieving balance with *material* kinetic energy, and if so, to what extent? The true answer exists independent of one's reality, and is solely based upon the actuality.

With respect to *motion*, there is a substantial paradox that lies in the characteristics of the two realms. If it is so stipulated that kinetic energy refers to "a thing" in *motion*; it is inescapable that in order for motion to exist, there must be both time and space. Even mere *vibration* as we know it, requires time and space; as well as "a thing" to move.

"A thing" cannot move without *space* in which to move. Velocity and speed each describe "a thing" that changes its location, with respect to time. Moreover; movement not only requires that "a thing" *be* in a particular "place;" but also that it is no longer in another, the "previous," place"—else movement from where?

It is true that speed generally refers to change in *distance*; and velocity refers to change in *displacement*. But even a circular movement back to the starting point, requires *distance*, even if final displacement is zero.

It is generally understood that: "Two objects cannot occupy the same space at the same time"—at least with respect to gross matter. Thus viewed from the other standpoint, even two neutrons simply cannot exist in a realm with no space. Atoms require space between the primary subatomic particles. Electrons must maintain space between themselves and the nucleus, and require space to orbit said nucleus; as do the celestial bodies.

Generally, this or the "immaterial realm," is considered as such and named as such, because it *does not* contain matter. However; it may in fact be the case that the immaterial realm simply *cannot* contain matter.

Bârâ, or true *creation*, as was done in early Genesis; could be considered as the initial release/conversion of immaterial *potential* energy *from* that which possesses it, *into* immaterial *kinetic* energy.

With *bârâ*, first there is this production of immaterial *kinetic* energy, as a function of the exercise of *will*. But also with bârâ, the desired result of this exercise of will, (particularly if matter); likely cannot exist in a realm with no space.

In order for this will to manifest, this energy; at least after Genesis 1:1; must be transferred to a realm where *space* exists.

After the exercise of this will, and just prior to this transfer of this energy to *this* realm, (the material), which "contains" space; there first exists immaterial *potential* energy, and then immaterial *kinetic* energy.

The problem now is the matter of *time*. There is no time in the realm where this initial process occurs. In fact; as previously stated, it could be reasonable argued that without the existence of time, the very concept of any type of *process* itself cannot possibly exist.

From the *material* perspective of a "hypothetical observer," there is or was the condition when whatever the initial *material* results of bârâ were *to be*; at some time prior to bârâ, the same *was not*.

Before the creation of that which God actually *created* after Genesis 1:1; there were no such entities or phenomena contained in the newly created *material* realm.

But from the *immaterial* perspective, there is no possible sequencing of these two or any other conditions, as there is no time available with which to sequence them.

Thus it seems that there is the choice between two dilemmas:

Either it was the case that the *causative* factor for the creation of a realm with time, space, and matter, somehow nevertheless existed in that same realm before the very realm itself existed—i.e.; the subset existed *prior* to the existence of the set in which it is or was contained.

Or; it is the case, that another realm exists from which this causative factor emanated; but with no ability in this same realm, to distinguish any temporal or spatial differences between when this cause existed as immaterial *potential* energy (prior to the exercise of will); and immaterial *kinetic* energy (the willful release of this potential).

Thus how can any differences be distinguished between the period of "time" when this *potential* energy existed, and *then* became *kinetic* while still in the immaterial; and then "subsequently" "bursting" into the material realm?

The "first one," Genesis 1:1 AKA the "Big Bang;" is a slight bit easier, as time did not yet exist "anywhere."

In fact; neither did any "where(s)" exist—at least as we know them.

But all of the *subsequent* immaterial kinetic energy *effects* in the material realm, must somehow comport with this time paradox. The material *effects* are separated by time on the *material* realm, (duration between events); yet the *causes* of these events exist in a realm with neither time nor space.

To make matters even more complex, again it seems likely that once this "happens;" i.e.; the material result is contained in the material realm; the original or any immaterial *potential* for this same "thing" is no longer contained in the immaterial realm.

It is not clear that a "no thing" in the immaterial realm, remains, or can remain in that realm; after this same "no thing" became "a thing" in the material realm.

This particular "no thing," is or was balanced by the appearance of "a thing," in the material.

This would explain why despite common belief, much of what was brought into existence in early Genesis, (after Genesis 1:1); was in fact not true creation or bârâ; and the correct translations, and even the various "versions," are consistent with this.

Thus the truth, is that given the fact that as a matter of logic, that since the first "possibility," (the existence of a subset or member of a set that does not yet exist), is simply impossible; it must therefore be ruled out.

Even if the "worlds without end," (*author's terminology*), position is taken; i.e.; "Big Bangs," then "contractions," and then new "Big Bangs," occur cyclically every ten billion years or so; there nevertheless remains that pesky matter of the first one.

Therefore the second; however *improbable*; must then necessarily represent the truth.

Simply because it appears that man is incapable of sufficiently *understanding* the immaterial realm, should in no way preclude his *attempting* to understand it. Neither should this preclude the establishment of working models—at least to the extent that that they in fact "work."

There are those who prefer to cling to the impossible—such as those who date the earth via the "Adam model" (*author's terminology*).

This position requires conflating or confusing Adam's *formation*, (yatsâr), from *something*, ('âphâr); with the *creation* (bârâ) of original hosts from *nothing*. But these adherents in fact represent the *only* proponents of an earth that is less than 10,000 years old, as the

Bible says no such thing. The same is likely the case here with their views regarding material-immaterial relationships.

One such "working model" from the *material* perspective, would be to establish one definition of *immaterial kinetic energy* as: "That which provides the means by which that which is in the *immaterial*, enters the *material*."

Bârâ or true creation is one example of this, but there are others.

Here "the thing" being "in motion," would not be with respect to *space* as is the case in the material realm; but rather would be "realm dependent."

When that which is in the immaterial realm as a *potential,* enters the material; this is the *kinetics* or motion.

Thus *immaterial kinetic*, is motion *between* the realms; i.e.; *immaterial* to *material*; rather than material kinetic motion *within* the *material* realm, as commonly understood.

Although it is interesting to ponder if so called "black holes," will ultimately be determined to be some type of "return path" mechanism from the material to the immaterial; this would represent mere speculation at this time.

John 14:12 (KJV) tells us:

> *"Verily, verily, I say unto you,*
> *He that believeth in me,*
> *the works that I do he shall do also;*
> *and greater works than these shall he do;*

because I go unto my father."[4]

It is clear and virtually undisputed that these "works" to which Jesus is referring, are not any woodworking projects He may have built as a child. Neither do they refer to any other types of *dynamikós* or *natural* power.

Rather; these "works" refer to *dunamis* or *supernatural* power, and thus the *miraculous* works He did. No mainstream religion disputes this, and the Book of Acts; which chronologically follows John; clearly confirms this meaning.

However with respect to other particulars contained in this passage, there are areas of significant dispute, which generally come down to two:

Firstly: it is often proffered that this passage refers to only the "Apostolic Era." Meaning; that what Jesus said, and to which He was clearly referring, had some type of "expiration" or "best if used before" date—e.g.; "Those were different times. Back then people could do those things—but not today."

There is no Biblical support whatsoever for this "Apostolic Era" position; thus the same likely merely represents an ineffective excuse for the lack of this, (dunamis), ability, on the part of the proponents of this position.

The *second* dispute is centered around the word "greater." Many proffer that what this actually means, is that since today there are so many more who "believe in Him and what He did;" there of course will be greater *numbers* of works, and that this in no way means works of greater *magnitude*.

However; the actual Greek word translated as "greater" that John used was:

> "3187 měizōn; irreg. compar. of 3173;
> larger..."⁵

It must be remembered that in here John 14:12 *měizōn* or "larger," is describing *works,* and not the *number* of works. Měizōn refers to *magnitude* of the works, and not the *quantity*.

It must also be noted that neither of the aforementioned disputes, seem to "dispute" *in-toto* the ability of man to engage in miraculous works.

One objects to the applicability today; and the other essentially objects to the idea that man could perform miraculous works that are *měizōn*, or larger than those performed by Jesus—despite the fact that Jesus Himself said so.

It is far beyond the scope of this work to explain the *mechanism* of what Jesus told us, particularly the last phrase: *"because I go unto my father."* [This mechanism is explained in great detail in an upcoming publication, currently in post-production.]

A *miracle* is something that occurs in the material realm, but is contrary to natural law.

In fact in order to be considered a miracle, it *must* contradict natural law or a laws; natural law here meaning the law or laws of the material realm.

If it does not contradict natural law via *supernatural* power, (dunamis), it is not a miracle, but represents merely natural power, (dynamikós)—no matter what it may otherwise seem to be.

A "miracle" is the transformation of immaterial potential energy, into immaterial kinetic energy, which then produces an *effect* in the material realm which defies natural law.

This is precisely what is happening in the early Genesis passages. It *is* the case, that all miracles are caused by immaterial kinetic energy; but it is *not* necessarily the case that all immaterial kinetic energy manifests as miracles in any absolute sense. As it is so that *material* kinetic energy has many manifestations, the same can be said about the manifestation of *immaterial* kinetic energy.

> *"When immaterial kinetic energy*
> *is imparted to the material realm,*
> *it is generally balanced by some type of*
> *motion in the material realm."*[6]
> —Emma B. Quadrakoff

In the case of bârâ or *creation*, this resultant motion exists at almost all levels, including the atomic and subatomic. All is in motion, with temperature being one way to indicate the amount of motion at the atomic or molecular level.

Absolute Zero is considered to be the temperature at which all such atomic and molecular motion ceases. It is not known if absolute zero exists or can exist anywhere in the material realm. In fact given current technology, it seems that in order to bring and particle of matter to absolute zero; a "freezer" capable of temperatures *below* absolute zero would both required and impossible.

In other material manifestations of *immaterial* kinetic energy, there is generally also some type of movement in the material realm.

Man is a dual being. We know this because of another passage in Genesis.

Genesis 2:7 tells us:

> "And God formed man from the dust of the ground, and breathed into his nostrils the breath of life; and man became a living soul."[7]

Although this is a description of how Adam was brought into existence, and not the original created hosts; the same rule applies today. The material vessel is first formed, and then God imparts His "breath" into the vessel. The condition of "physical life" begins with the first breath, and ends with the last.

Thus while "physically alive," man has both a *material* and an *immaterial* component. One is *indirectly* of God, (material); and the other is *directly* of God, (immaterial); often described as *body* and *soul* respectively.

The *material* part is subject to the laws of the material realm, unless acted upon by an immaterial force; e.g.; immaterial kinetic energy. And the *immaterial* part is subject to the laws of the immaterial realm.

Most religions speak of, and are very concerned with "afterlife." This is what happens *after-life*; with life being defined here as that dual condition, or the unity of body and soul. Afterlife is that *severed* condition; and that which happens to the *immaterial* portion, after it is no longer contained within the physical vessel.

But again, when speaking of the realm that has no time; that realm, by definition, has "no time." This is not meant as any type of tautology, but rather as a reminder. If there is no time; then from the immaterial perspective, one could just as easily inquire as to "beforelife," or that condition of this immaterial portion *before* it is "breathed into his nostrils. . . and man became (becomes) a living soul."

Physical, (material), nostrils are required before they can be "breathed into." It seems that the only time that "time" affects this *immaterial* portion, is when it is contained in the physical vessel. "Beforelife" is rarely spoken about by conventional religions.

In very real senses, biology, the study of (the physical portion) of life, is in actuality a study of *miracles*; in that life within certain limits, defies natural law. But we tend to not notice this, because life is so ubiquitous.

The material changes that occur to a corpse, are *consistent* with natural law. The material changes that occur regularly to a living being generally *defy* this natural law. If a corpse is damaged, it remains damaged. If the same body was damaged while alive, it would repair itself; and reverse the damage, again within certain limits. The latter represents an unusual *effect* or a series of *effects*, and thus requires an unusual cause.

The reason or *cause* of this, is what is known as the *Vital Life Force* (VLF) by some, *chi* by others, or *Innate Intelligence* by certain professionals. This "energy" provides the mechanism by which living beings maintain homeostasis; maintaining or increasing the levels of organization of the material body. When this energy is interfered with either *materially*, [see *chiropractic*]; or immaterially, [see: the Monograph: "*It's Not Just a Theory*"); less than optimal organization is the result.

This VLF is another form of immaterial kinetic energy. The origin is the *immaterial* realm; its target is in the *material* realm; and its *purpose* is the maintenance of the *material* vessel that contains the immaterial portion; i.e.; maintaining the physical part of that dual condition of "life."

As previously stated, the VLF is capable of being interfered with immaterially, *before* reception by the material target; and interfered with materially, *after* reception by the target.

Areas of the nervous system are currently believed to be the intended material recipient of this VLF. Much like a radio receiver receiving *material* electromagnetic waves, and converting the same into that which can be understood; parts of the nervous system represent that junction between the *immaterial* VLF, and the material. That intelligence which is needed to maintain the physical body is received from the *immaterial*, and converted into the *material*, by parts of the nervous system.

As an aside; that which is referred to as *spirit*, although often used synonymously for "anything immaterial," is similar to the VLF; but solely with respect to *inanimate* matter.

"Spirit" is technically that *immaterial* phenomenon which either gives or gave the material existence; and/or that which *maintains* the existence of the material. When the immaterial kinetic energy that created the universe manifested, was this energy flow a "one time" event; or does this energy continue to flow? This is difficult to comprehend; much less answer; as it also emanates from this realm with no time.

Before there was the material realm, there was not a material realm. As previously stated, the *cause* of the material realm therefore could not have been contained in the yet to be created material realm.

The same can be said of *natural* law, or the laws of the *material* realm. Natural law or the laws of the material realm therefore also had to first exist in the immaterial; else whence did they originate?

Hence one meaning of: "As above so below."

Perhaps a hackneyed expression, but nevertheless one which essentially contains as much revelation as one is willing to seek. It really could not be any other way. Perhaps another phrasing of this concept would be: "Thy will be done, on earth, as it is in heaven;" here with heaven meaning the immaterial realm, and not "the heavens," or the "space" between the celestial bodies. This is usually approached from a bit of a different angle though, because it is phrased in a manner suggesting that it is hoped or desired that God's will be done here on earth, in the same way and manner as it is done in heaven.

All that was *originally* brought into physical existence; was brought into existence because of, and completely consistent with; the will of God. Thus from the other viewpoint, when examining the known physical realm as the accomplished *result* of God's will, this physical realm necessarily was already done on earth as it is or was in heaven, according to His will—at least through the end of Genesis 1:1.

Therefore, the physical laws we know to exist on earth, necessarily have their origins in the will of God. For each physical law, then there must be a corresponding law in the non-physical or immaterial; which some might choose to use the term supernatural, realm.

> *"Any action which is preceded by conscious thought, is a two-fold phenomenon; having both material and immaterial components."*[8]
> —Emma B. Quadrakoff

In Malachi 3:10 (NAS) God tells us:

> *"Bring the whole tithe into the storehouse, so that there may be food in My house, and test Me now in this," says the LORD of hosts,*

> *"if I will not open for you the*
> *windows of heaven*
> *and pour out for you a*
> *blessing until it overflows."*[9]

The most striking words or phrase in this passage is the phrase "test Me." God does not state that we are to examine or quiz Him, but rather to "test" (*bachan*)[10] Him. This is not an invitation to inquire as to the nature of God. Neither is it an invitation to quiz Him to see how much he knows; but rather is an invitation to actually test Him.

This "test," is in the sense of finding out not if He actually is what *we* say He is; but rather if He is actually what *He* says He is. This is similar to the acid tests for testing precious metals such as gold. In those tests, one is generally trying to determine if the metal is actually what the metal is being proffered to be.

The nature of this "test" involves the very same physical principles or laws we encounter in our everyday existence:

The following may at first appear very complicated, but is not. For some reason, many people seem to become intimidated when confronted with symbols.

Nevertheless, the following is really quite simple:

> "Newton's Second Law of Motion" states:
> *"The acceleration of an object*
> *as produced by a net force*
> *is directly proportional to the*
> *magnitude of the net force,*

INEVITABLE BALANCE

in the same direction as the net force, and inversely proportional to the mass of the object."[11]

All this really means; is that if you push on something with enough force, it will move in the direction in which you pushed it. It is expressed as F = MA, where F = force, M = mass, and A = acceleration.

It really is that simple. Push on a mass, (M), with a force, (F); and it will move (A). And the greater the mass, the slower it will move given the same force.

When something is moving, it has either velocity or speed. This is a change in the distance it travels in a certain amount of time. A car traveling 60 MPH will travel sixty miles in one hour. (*$v=\Delta d/\Delta t$ velocity or speed equals change in distance or displacement divided by the change in time; for speed and velocity respectively.*)

In order to make an object such as a car, (or a blessing), change its speed or velocity; this requires some type of acceleration. This acceleration, or A, is considered to be the change in the object's speed or velocity. This happens when one pushes down on either the gas pedal, (accelerator), in a car; or the brakes. The gas pedal provides *positive* acceleration, and the car increases its speed or velocity. The brakes provide *negative* acceleration, (deceleration); and will slow the car down. (*$A=\Delta v/\Delta t$ acceleration equals change in speed or velocity divided by the change in time*)

F = MA simply tells us that force equals mass multiplied by acceleration. All this really means, is that if the object is a large mass; then it takes more force to accelerate it, (change its velocity or speed), a given amount; as compared to a smaller mass. If the mass is small, and it is subject to the same force, its acceleration will be greater.

When the car is carrying a heavy load, the gas pedal has to be pushed farther down in order to get more force from the engine to cause the car to increase its speed, (accelerate), as compared to an empty vehicle. Although not technically exactly correct, if we consider the weight of the car to be M, this is all that F = MA means. *(Technically mass and weight are different, but this matters little here.)*

The "test" in the passage from Malachi previously cited, refers to 4 things:

1) the *window*
2) the *tithe*
3) the *blessing*
4) the *pouring*

The *window* is a binary, in that it must be either open or closed. It is essentially *allegorical*, as it is far from certain that literal windows, at least as we know them to be; actually exist in heaven. This "window," essentially means merely a route for something to travel from the immaterial to the material.

Assuming this route exists, meaning the window is open; this leaves the *tithe*, the *blessing* and the *pouring*. These can be expressed in the terms of Newton's second law, F = MA or more specifically here, F_T = MA where:

F_T = total value of faith
M = the quantity of the blessing (how much stuff)
A = the pouring or movement. (the increase in velocity of the blessing from zero, to some speed or velocity) This determines how fast the blessing will get to you.

The "test" referred to in this example from Malachi, refers to the *results* of tithing. F_T or total faith value in this context is essentially "putting your money where your mouth is." It is equal to the *amount* you tithe, multiplied by the *reasons* for which you tithe; or, more simply put; how much did you tithe, and why did you tithe it.

Here is the where the: "*Any action which is preceded by conscious thought, is a two-fold phenomenon; having both material and immaterial components,*" rule comes into play. In the case of tithing in Malachi; there is both the *tithe*, and the *reason* for the tithe.

The *tithe*, (amount), itself is essentially a *material* phenomenon. One donates the fruits of ones labor to that which they believe should be the recipient, according to God's instructions in Malachi. This action is essentially *material kinetic* energy, resulting in *material potential* energy in the earthly recipient. The recipient now has this new material potential energy, which can ultimately be converted into material kinetic energy, by utilization of the material value of this tithe to produce change.

The *reason* for the tithe is an *immaterial* quantity. Once the tithe is given, (becomes kinetic), as per the will of the giver; both the *amount* of the tithe and the *reasons* for the tithe; (F_T); become *immaterial* kinetic energy released into the immaterial realm.

This release initially produces an imbalance in the immaterial realm, and ultimately results in immaterial *potential* energy.

Since kinetic energy relates to *motion*; and motion requires both *distance* and *time*; it is unclear as to how this could possibly remain kinetic in a realm that has neither.

This immaterial *potential* energy balances the original immaterial imbalance caused by the F_T. And the same as a charged battery, this potential remains an *unbalanced* immaterial phenomenon, ready to be released.

Thus as stated, the giving of the tithe produces both material and immaterial *imbalances*:

In the *material* realm, the *material* amount of the tithe results in increased potential energy to the recipient of the tithe in the *material* realm; and this increase is commensurate with the amount of the tithe. Said recipient can now make material changes by converting this now material potential energy, into material kinetic energy; with this subsequent action, (spending or consuming), subject to his, (the recipient's), will.

At the same time in the immaterial realm, the *immaterial* amount of the tithe—which is the *amount* of the tithe and the *reasons* for the tithe; ultimately results in increased potential energy in the *immaterial* realm—essentially with the "tither's" name written upon it.

Two different *material* quantities or amounts, have two different *immaterial* quantities or contributions to the total. The subsequent conversion of this immaterial potential energy, into immaterial *kinetic* energy, is subject to His, (God's), will.

We generally can easily calculate the material *amount* we tithe; but this multiplier, here meaning the value of the actual *reasons* for tithing, which are also necessary for determining the total amount which F_T represents; can only be calculated by God.

Perhaps a better way to describe this, would be that the value of the faith total is calculated in this manner: $F_T = F_A \times F_R$ The faith subscript "A" represents the *amount* of a tithe or other "good works;" and subscript "R" represents the *reasons*. The value of this F_R, is the factor by which the thirty fold, sixty fold, and one hundred+ fold realms are calculated. Matthew 13:8 provides insight into these realms of increase.

This reason, or "why factor" is extremely important. This is not only because this factor largely determines the *quantity* of the blessing; but also because of our *material* limitations for the actual amount, (how much), of the giving.

One cannot reasonably give more than 100% of what one has. In the tithing example, even if one tithed all of their increase instead of the required 10%, this in itself would result in only a tenfold increase in the blessing. But the *reason* or why factor could easily result in a return in the "hundred fold realm."

This concept is further illustrated by Proverbs 16:2 (NAS), where it tells us:

J. Bartholomew Walker

> *"All the ways of a man are clean
> in his own sight,
> But the LORD weighs the motives."*[12]

Weight is actually a force. (Weight itself, is technically a function of mass, and the acceleration of gravity.) Proverbs is telling us here, that God determines, (*"weighs"*), the value of the motives or reasons. This *is* the F_R.

"Weighing" something, is generally determining the resultant force of its mass, multiplied by the acceleration of gravity.

In the F = MA equation, M is being used here to represent the blessing; or precisely what it is that travels through this "window," from the immaterial to the material.

The use of the term "Blessing" here means: "increase *consistent* with natural law." This is to be distinguished from "increase *inconsistent* with natural law," which is better termed a "miracle."

This in no way means that miracles cannot be a result of tithing; but rather only that in Malachi, it is *blessings* which are under discussion.

"A" represents the actual acceleration, resulting in the movement or pouring out of this blessing. This acceleration is actually the direct result of God's intervention.

"Newton's First Law of Motion" states:

INEVITABLE BALANCE

> *"An object at rest stays at rest*
> *and an object in motion stays in motion*
> *with the same speed*
> *and in the same direction*
> *unless acted upon by an unbalanced force."*[13]

This essentially means that an object that is moving, will stay moving; unless acted upon by another force. Or an object that is not moving, will continue to not move; unless a sufficient force is applied to make it move.

This, (not moving), is the initial status of the M, or the blessings, (potential energy), which are in heaven. They are already there, but will not move or change their direction of movement unless a force is applied.

For those who might argue that these blessings might already be moving; it would seem that if this were so, then said movement is definitely not towards this window, or God would merely open the window, and would not have to pour them out. Thus, let's assume they are stationary.

In order to move, they must have a change in velocity from zero to something. For any mass; any change in velocity with respect to time represents an *acceleration*, and this requires a *force*.

It is the conversion of the immaterial *potential* energy into immaterial *kinetic* energy, that provides this force, and determines the magnitude of the "blessing."
As previously stated:

> *"Any action which is preceded by conscious thought,*

*is a two-fold phenomenon; having
both material and immaterial components."*

Following is a representation of this "two-fold" phenomenon:

(Amount) → Material Kinetic → Material Potential → Eventual Material Kinetic

Tithing → ↕

(Amount and Reason) → Immaterial Kinetic → Immaterial Potential → Eventual Immaterial Kinetic

Here is where Newton's Third Law of Motion comes into play:

*"For every action, there is an
equal and opposite reaction."*[14]

Newton's Third Law of Motion probably represents the most fundamental law of compensation, or "karma."

When the value of F_T is established, this represents the force of faith, which we cause by tithing or giving; this being something which is always done for some type of reason. The amount or value of the gift (F_A) is one factor; the other being the reason (F_R) we are doing it.

INEVITABLE BALANCE

It must be clearly stated here that the value of this reason is not necessarily the reason we may tell others; and it is not necessarily the reason we tell ourselves. Rather; it is based upon the true reasons, which God always knows no matter what we may say or do; and it is God alone who "weighs" these.

Thus here this F_T represents the first action as referenced in Newton's third law. When this action is consummated; when we tithe; an equal but opposite reaction is undertaken by God, being "paid for" with the immaterial potential/kinetic energy of the F_T. This results in another $F = MA$.

Again it is important to remember that it is not just how much we give alone; but the value of that gift *and* the "reason" multiplier, which determines the total value of this force.

This A, (change in velocity), of M, (the blessing); is the result of the equal and opposite action undertaken by God, as a direct result of our actions. It is equal to His calculation of F_T, but "opposite" in direction, as now; instead of going *from* us, it travels *to* us.

The rest of the *second*, ($F = MA$), equation also holds. The acceleration is inversely proportional to the mass of the object. In the physical world this means that given whatever the total force applied may be; the greater the mass, the less the acceleration, and the slower the resultant movement to you. Likewise: the lesser the mass; the greater the acceleration, and the faster the resultant movement toward you.

This same relationship holds in the immaterial realm. The mathematical product of this God induced MA, must remain constant; and is equal to, but is opposite in direction to, the original F_T, (original tithe and reasons), for this particular event.

Thus, the *greater* the blessing you are to receive, the *longer* it may take to get to you. If the blessing is received *quickly*, the *amount* or mass of the blessing is sacrificed or diminished in exchange for the rapidity with which it is received. This is necessary to keep the equation in balance.

How does God decide whether to provide a smaller blessing quickly, or a larger blessing more slowly?

Only He knows this for sure, but in the initial stages of faith, rapidity can be very important; as it is evidence to the "neophyte" that the system actually works. Once the system is known to work; even with a relatively small amount of increase, but an extremely rapid increase; the system becomes confirmed as functional by the believer. Thus he or she is much more likely to permit this to ascend to higher levels.

With subsequent tithing or giving, as the amount of one's faith, (God passed this test), increases; then God may choose to increase the magnitude of M at the expense of A; but again this must equal the new F_T.

This is a different result, (more quantity of blessing, or M), than the above ""rapid" process; but God's priorities may be different. With this increased *quantity* of blessing, the acceleration will be *less* in order to balance the F=MA equation. This means the velocity or speed of the blessing will be *less*, and subsequently this *greater* amount of blessing will take *longer* to arrive.

Whenever this results in a much greater, but slower to arrive, blessing being returned; of course the enemy knows this. He, (the enemy), has a way to sense when "due season" is near. During those dry periods, when it looks like God forgot all about you, and it appears that He isn't doing a thing; this is the dangerous period. That is when your faith is attacked, and it is not *examined* but actually "tested."

The enemy will remark with something like: "See, God aint gonna do nuthin. If God was gonna do sumthin, he (sic.) would have done it by now."

Is this because the devil does not know of this $F = MA$ function? No, it is because he knows precisely of this function.

All the while this huge mass of blessing is heading toward you with a relatively slow acceleration having been applied; but with the magnitude of this mass or blessing being beyond your ability to think or imagine. The devil likely can sense this, and he is trying desperately to get you to do something; to get you to do *anything* that will cancel out your receipt of this blessing.

To be clear, all of this is not about storing up blessings in heaven; but rather in the here and now, in this *material* plane—most particularly, if the F_A is in any way material in nature.

This $F = MA$ law is not unique to tithing. Rather, it applies to any action or inaction undertaken; and is sometimes referred to as *karma*.

Anything we choose to do, or not do; has quantities that are calculable and the same rules apply. We should do unto others as we should do unto ourselves if for no other reason; because that is precisely what *will* be done unto us; and done according to the aforementioned rules.

If something is undertaken for this, (the *return* or "gimmee the money"), reason alone however; the value of F_T, and the subsequent value of the returning MA, is likely to be smaller; as the reason or motive value is diminished if it is largely a selfish act.

2 Corinthians 9:7 (NAS) tells us:

> *"Each one must do just as he
> has purposed in his heart,
> not grudgingly or under compulsion,
> for God loves a cheerful giver."*[15]

Why does God love a cheerful giver? Because it is His will that we prosper; and this gives Him license, arguably *requires* Him, to bless us not only based upon what we do; but more importantly why we do it.

This law cannot be changed; neither can it be avoided. It makes little difference what we say the weight of our motives are, as we are not "*in charge*" of weighing or calculating them; and thus our opinion of their value is essentially irrelevant.

One very reliable way to short circuit this process is to name your own blessing. If boasting about the amount of the tithe, (or whatever it may be), is undertaken; that is precisely what can easily happen.

INEVITABLE BALANCE

Malachi 3:10 is about the *positive*. Meaning: that it is *blessings* that are the subject, as they relate to tithing. However the same rules apply with respect to so called "cursing."

Thus, if and when the F_T is "negative," the MA must also be "negative" in nature.

As previously stated, man has no choice but to act from the standpoint of *reality*. Man *by design*, is simply incapable of the perception of material actuality *in-toto*. Man's ability to hear is dwarfed by the hearing ability of canines or raccoons. Man's vision is arguably no more than an octave. Man's olfactory capabilities are dwarfed by those possessed by a deer. Taste is limited, and tactile discrimination leaves much to be desired. And all of man's senses are subject to error— the aforementioned mirage and a computer display being prime examples. Thus man is forced to act based upon what he *believes* is true.

The Solipsists have a valid point, when they state that the only thing one knows for *certain*, is that they; (the Solipsist); exist. Phrased another way; one's "I am," is all that is actually "known."

Why is it that one cannot obtain a positive F_T, simply by doing something negative, for terrible reasons?

For example: "I hated him, and wanted to really hurt him; so I stole money from him." Here it seems that the product of the *negative action*, and the *negative* reasons should be a *positive*. After all, a negative multiplied by a negative, does in fact yield a positive product. "It's not the case that I don't have any money," means one *has* money.

To understand this, another question must be asked. What number is it that is the most similar to the number 3? Most would answer that 2.99999... *ad infinitum* would be the answer.

But the truth; is that the number most similar to 3 is −3. The magnitude is exactly the same, but the direction is opposite; with each being exactly the same distance from zero on a number line—with the *absolute values* being equal. A $3.00 account receivable to one; represents a $3.00 payable to another. The quantitative actuality is exactly the same.

The amount of money "stolen from him," has an actuality independent of where it is or how it got there. If this money fell out of the thief's pocket, and was found by another; the "finder" would have no idea as to how it was obtained.

The fact that a car was stolen instead of purchased, has no effect whatsoever on the actuality of the car. There is no way to tell the difference between a stolen actuality; and the same actuality obtained legally, simply by examining the actuality.

If thieves believed that a $3.00 theft would ultimately become -$3.00, no one would ever steal. But it is worse, as the truth is that said $3.00 theft in actuality has a value of $\geq$ -$3.00; where here the "greater than" means increase in the "amount owed." How much more than $3.00 is "owed," depends upon the magnitude of the *reason* (F_R) for the theft.

If somehow one in actuality stole this same amount, but was genuinely unaware that they were stealing it; this does not mean they get to keep it. It merely means that only the amount that was equal to the amount stolen will be taken from them; hence the use of ≥ - $3.00, rather than merely greater than.

Being dual in nature, man is also designed with *immaterial* capabilities. Reception of the VLF, (Vital Life Force); is in certain senses autonomic, (as in autonomy), or automatic; but man is designed to receive much more than this from the immaterial realm.

However; unlike the VLF, these other capabilities are *not* necessarily automatic. Other than the VLF and some rudimentary capabilities; many of man's immaterial capabilities must be *developed*. There are some exceptions to this in those who either were born with these capabilities, or obtained them suddenly. But for most people most of the time, these capabilities must be developed.

It is the case with military secrets; that once an enemy knows that something *can* be done; said enemy will spend any and all necessary resources in order to find a way to also do it. This is precisely why the mere *existence* of various weapons is highly classified.

A similar condition exists with man's *immaterial* capabilities. The enemy knows that the very best way to stop any H. Sapien from developing their immaterial capabilities; is to make certain that no H. Sapien ever finds out that which is *possible*.

There is no political or religious bias required in order to state that there is, and has been, a "war on

Christianity" in the United States for some time. Reasonable "objective observation" alone will prove that this is clearly a fact.

It must be asked *why* such a war exists? Is it merely a matter of ideology, or is there more than this involved. After all, the United States is largely a Christian country, founded on Judeo-Christian (and Masonic) principles.

The answer to this question has already been provided, but will be restated here.

Again, John 14:12 (KJV) tells us:

> *"Verily, verily, I say unto you,*
> *He that believeth in me, the works*
> *that I do he shall do also;*
> *and greater works than these shall*
> *he do; because I go unto my father."*[16]

Christians can and do debate "what this means," despite the unmistakable clarity. Christians can invent all sorts of explanations as to why this passage; again just as in the fact that Adam could *not* possibly be the first man; does not mean what it so clearly states. But nevertheless, the forces of darkness know precisely what it means.

Those same forces of darkness know very well what would happen to them; *if* Christians understood this passage, and began to do something about it. After all, "Christ" was not Jesus' last name; but rather refers to him as *The* "Anointed One." It is because of the anointing of the *third* part of the Trinity, upon the *second* part of Trinity that resulted in this "eponymous" quasi-surname.

Thus true *Christianity*, is largely about the *Christos*, or the anointing of the Holy Ghost. The source of the term *Christianity* itself refers to the *third* part of the Trinity. Were this not so; "Jesusite" would likely have been the term chosen. Although no human can ever be *The* Anointed One, every human being can be *an* anointed one; and we are told one way to do this in the above John 14:12.

This in no way represents any attempt to minimize the importance of Jesus. Salvation/redemption/justification is really a two-part process. With respect to the first part, or Jesus' contribution: "It is finished." And with respect to the second part, this requires nothing more than each "man's" acceptance of this fact.

But Jesus clearly was about a lot more than man's salvation/redemption/justification—as important as this is. And without Jesus, not only would man still be waiting for a "Redeemer;" but the power increase Jesus spoke of in John 14:12 would not be available to man.

Today most representations of Jesus are either as a baby, or on the cross. This is done deliberately in an attempt to minimize Him. But one only need read about Him to understand that there is much more to Him than this.

Jesus was also a teacher—hence the term *Rabbi* or *Rabboni*. He taught much about how the "system" works, and how we should behave—with the former explaining why the latter. He provides the perfect role model for each of us.

Jesus also worked miracles, and assured us that each of us, that not only could we perform equal works, but *greater* works than He; *if* one merely met the criteria, *and* He went to the Father.

In certain ways, Jesus existed at a time similar to today. Many believe that outside of the practical concerns of those He helped, that the main reason for His performing of miracles was the fulfillment of prophesy—so that all would know who He is or was.

This is an interesting position, and worthy of some analysis:

If it is believed that the miracles Jesus performed, were alone to uniquely prove Him to be the Messiah; this is simply *not true*.

The truth is that many of the miracles He performed, had already been performed by others, and performed long before His birth. If the ability to perform miracles were the only criteria for being the Messiah; then Elijah, "double dose" Elisha, as well as others, could also qualify. Heck; a dead man jumped back to life after his body merely touched the bones of a long deceased Elisha.

The position should not be that of believing that Jesus performed these miracles primarily or simply to fulfill prophesy, even though that did in fact happen. The position should be based upon the answer to a question. The same being: "Why was this or were these prophesied?"

In other words: Outside of helping some individuals; why was it necessary for Jesus to perform these miracles, many of which had already been performed by others long before his birth?

The answer is a mere two words: *"They forgot!"*

The Father *knew beforehand*, that by the time of the birth of Jesus, His chosen people would have forgotten much regarding that which had been written. If it is stipulated that Malachi represents the end of the Old Testament, then the end of the Old Testament was written roughly five hundred years prior to Jesus' birth.

This represents a substantial period of time for the enemy to "work" His, (God's), people; utilizing the old "literal to allegory" trick—a particularly effective tool when dealing with miracles performed a very long time ago.

Knowing this, and always economizing; He, (God), instructed His prophets to include these miracles as parts of those prophesies written prior to Jesus' birth. Thus although Jesus had to perform these miracles to fulfill the prophesy; the true reason for their inclusion in the prophesy was education, or perhaps *re-education*—used here in its original benign meaning.

Thus it seems fair to say, that Jesus did not have the unique capability to perform most of the miracles He performed prior to His "death" because He was Jesus. Rather that because He was Jesus, He was to perform miracles primarily to educate or *re-educate*, and to fulfill prophesy only as a secondary matter. [One exception to this; is or was Jesus' "resurrection without recourse"—perhaps a unique event in the history of man.]

It is obvious that so many today have fallen for the aforementioned "literal to allegory" trick. Here what is *literal* in the Bible; is over time believed to be *allegorical*. In actuality, this represents "cutting a deal."

There are those who ascribe "facts" to the Bible that cannot possibly be true—the age of the earth, and "no such thing as evolution" being prime examples. [*It is true that original man was created (bârâ), and thus this (the creation of man) was not the result of any evolutionary process. However this in no way precludes any subsequent evolution of man. Neither does this preclude any subsequent evolution of any other created life forms.*]

Maintaining these impossible positions as "Bible facts;" as is also the legal case with a witness who has lied; impeaches the credibility of the entire Word. This is particularly heinous, because the Bible does not even remotely state any such things. No references for these positions exist outside of the minds of their proponents.

But there is an *emotional* need to believe that the Bible is true, so here comes the "deal." Just as Tom Sawyer did with respect to the pirates in the cave; we'll "let on" that the Bible is not to be taken too literally, and those things such as miracles are merely allegorical.

And since any "allegory" is useless without explanation, any said attempts at explanation can make little or no sense, as the foundation of this is falsehood.

It is fair to say that *the Bible as originally written*, represents God according to *God*.

It is also fair to say that *religion*, represents God according to *man*.

INEVITABLE BALANCE

Thus when the Bible does not support a religious tenet; it is the meaning of the Bible that is changed to conform—with this; [Adam was the first created man, and the subsequent incorrect age of the earth]; being merely one example.

Freemasonry is currently guilty of the exact opposite. Freemasonry is often defined as: "A system of morality, veiled in *allegory*, and illustrated by symbols."

Here Freemasons are *told* that by definition, that much of what is contained in Freemasonry is by design *allegory*, in order to facilitate concealment—largely because of prosecutions over the centuries.

Yet most nevertheless teach it as *literal*, and thus having no additional significance beyond flowery words. The "working tools," as *symbols* utilized for illustration, remain somewhat intact; but even these "meanings," are also slowly being changed over time.

The truth; is that Biblical *stories* that contain actual names are actual stories. One is certainly free to believe that any given story is true, or that the story is false. But no license exists to change the *intention* of the writer from literal to allegorical. The writers of these *stories* meant their works to be taken literally—irrespective of whether *believed* or not.

The *parables* contained in the Bible are there to teach principles, but do not necessarily represent actual events that actually occurred. The "Talent Man" story is a parable, albeit generally misunderstood today. [See Monograph #603 "*Donald Trump Candidacy According to Matthew?*" for the true explanation of this parable.]

This "Talent Man" *parable*, is not a *recollection* of any actual persons; but rather a means by which a system is being taught. The truth is that most people at sometime in their lives have behaved exactly like the one talent man. This was also the case at the time Jesus told the parable; which is precisely why He told it, and why it was memorialized.

By the deliberate altering of that which is *literal*, to that which is considered as *allegorical*; the *realities* of the *actualities* recounted in the Bible are likewise changed. And as previously mentioned, humans must always act from their realities, as there is no other choice.

According to the Bible, there was an actuality known as Legion. The *story* of Legion is neither a *parable*, nor an *allegory*. And as Jesus *literally* stated, and since He already went to the Father; today those who believe in Him and the things that He did, are *literally* capable of even greater things than these.

There is a passage in Matthew that merits extremely serious consideration. Here in this similar but different *story* than Legion, (is not a *parable*); the disciples had attempted to cast a demon out of a boy, but were unsuccessful.

The boy's father then brought the boy to Jesus to cast out the demon, and He, (Jesus), was successful. The disciples then inquired of Jesus as to why it was that they had failed.

Following is Matthew 17:14-19 according to *The King James Version*:

> *"And when they were come*
> *to the multitude,*

INEVITABLE BALANCE

*There came to him a certain man, kneeling
down to him, and saying, Lord, have
mercy on my son:
for he is lunatick, and sore vexed:
for oft times he falleth into the fire,
and oft into the water.*

*And I brought him to thy disciples,
and they could not cure him.*

*Then Jesus answered and said,
O faithless and perverse generation,
how long shall I be with you?
how long shall I suffer you?
bring him hither to me.
And Jesus rebuked the devil;
and he departed out of him:
and the child was cured from
that very hour.*

*Then came the disciples to Jesus apart,
and said, Why could not we cast him out?"*[17]

Matthew 17 verses 20-22 (KJV), then tell us:

20 "*And Jesus said unto them,
Because of your unbelief;
for verily I say unto you,
If ye have faith as a grain of mustard seed,
ye shall say unto this mountain,
Remove hence to yonder place;*

*and it shall remove; and nothing
shall be impossible unto you."*[18]

→21 *"Howbeit this kind goeth
not out but by prayer and fasting."*[19] ←

*"And while they abode in Galilee,
Jesus said unto them, 'The Son of man
shall be betrayed into the hands of men:'"*[20]

The word "howbeit," which appears in verse 21; is not equivalent to: "How be it?;" which would then represent a *question*.

Rather; "howbeit" generally means "however;" representing a *statement* such as "nevertheless." This "nevertheless" represents an attempt to modify what was just stated rule in verse 20, for this particular situation. Thus this is represented as Jesus *answering* a question, and not the disciples *asking* another question.

Verse 20 has to do with that which is immaterial; here unbelief, and as will be seen is sometimes also translated as insufficient "faith."

But the inclusion of verse 21 completely negates what Jesus just stated in the preceding verse regarding unbelief or insufficient faith being *causative*; by stating in 21: "(nevertheless) *this kind not goeth out but by prayer and fasting.*" The "but" here could also be reasonably translated as "except."

INEVITABLE BALANCE

It seems peculiar that Jesus would answer the disciples' question as He did in verse 20; and then in the very next verse tell them that all He just said in the previous verse did not apply in this case.

And this is especially odd, because the original question He was asked was about this specific matter. So as it reads, Jesus must then have first answered a question about something else entirely different; and then went on to answer the question he was actually asked, negating what He had just said about other matters of which He was not asked.

In addition, there is the matter of lack of specificity. In verse 20, Jesus speaks of the relative *quantities* of a "*mustard seed,*" (cause); and a moving mountain, (effect). Yet; there is no mention in verse 21 of how much praying, or how much fasting is required.

And it is clear that verse 22 begins an entirely different matter that is unrelated to that which precedes it.

Following is Matthew 17:20-22; but here according to the *New American Standard Bible*:

20 "*And He said unto them,*
"*Because of the littleness of your faith;*
for truly I say to you,
if you have faith the size of a mustard seed,
you will say to this mountain,
"*Move from here to there," and it will move;*
and nothing will be impossible to you."[21]

→21 ["*But this kind does not go out*

J. Bartholomew Walker

> *except by prayer and fasting."]*[22]←
>
> 22 *"And while they were gathering together
> in Galilee Jesus said to them,
> 'The Son of Man is going to be delivered
> into the hands of men;'"*[23]

The most notable difference here in the NAS version, is the inclusion of *brackets*. According to NAS: "[] = In text, brackets indicate words probably not in the original writings."[24]

So although clearly this passage appears in the KJV; it is likewise included in the NAS, but with the caveat that it is "probably not in the original writings."

But given the presence of verse 21 in each of these two popular "versions," surely it must have come from somewhere. It seems that although it is not known whence verse 21 came, it is known whence it did not—the original writings, at least according to NAS.

This leaves only writings that are *not original* as any possible source. It must also be remembered that this is a *story*, and these passages represent an eyewitness account.

Following is Matthew 17:20-22; but here according to the *New International Version Bible*:

> 20 *"He replied, "Because you so little faith.
> I tell you the truth, if you have
> faith as small as a mustard seed,
> you can say to this mountain,*

*'Move from here to there' and it will move."
Nothing will be impossible for you."*[25]

→21 *(No verse is present—nothing.)*[26]←

22 *"When they came together Galilee,
he said to them, 'The Son of Man
is going to be betrayed into the hands of
men.'"*[27]

Much like the "thirteenth floor" on many buildings; here in the NIV, there is no 21st verse present in Matthew 17. Matthew 17 simply goes from verse 20, to verse 22; with no verse 21.

The difference here is that many buildings in fact do actually have a thirteenth floor; it is just called something else—meaning that there is the actuality of a floor 13 stories up, it is just *called* something different.

But here in Matthew, it is *not* a matter of these words existing, and merely a difference of opinion as to where they appear, or what they are numbered. Rather, there is disagreement as to whether or not Jesus actually ever spoke these words. Thus the existence of this very actuality itself is in question.

It should be asked precisely who or what non-"original" source would have added verse 21; and for what specific reason(s)?

Although it is not possible to ascertain the particular *source* of this particular "verse;" nevertheless, (*howbeit*), some *reasons* for this "addition" can be logically derived.

In verse 20, it is clear that Jesus is speaking of *belief* or *faith* that provides the means by which this enemy is cast out. This means that the source of this power is *the individual* that is directly involved in the casting out.

It is the *will* of the individual, along with *faith* that provides the F; and the MA is the subsequent exit of the demon; with the M here being considered as the demon, and the A the movement out.

But if verse 21 were true, then this would mean that a tiny force that is capable of moving a mountain; would somehow nevertheless be insufficient for casting out a demon.

And more importantly; here in verse 21, the source of the power becomes *indirect*.

Meaning; that here it is no longer the will of the individual along with faith that *directly* provides the actuality of F, and the subsequent MA of the exit of the demon.

Instead; this "fasting" and "prayer" merely provide an immaterial imbalance, (*potential*); which is then, (hopefully), balanced by God; by *Him* providing the F and subsequent MA causing the exit, (*kinetic*), of the demon.

The hierarchy is God, man, and then all else. This "all else" includes angels and demons. Angels must obey man's will, unless man's will conflicts with God's will. When man's will and God's will conflict; God's will necessarily prevails.

Since a fair argument exists that demons are or were actually angels, the same rule applies. Whenever a human is possessed by a demon, this is not God's will. But unfortunately, this is much more complex than it seems.

Up to a certain point, just as was the case with the *attacks* on Job; demonic *possession* is also often possible, because of the previous actions of the "host."

This *possession*, is part of the balancing of the actuality of the host's free will from previous willful actions. Simply because this may not be a part of any given host's *reality* regarding any given willful action, this in no way means it is not so. In these cases, it is merely another part of the *actuality* of the totality of the action. [See Monograph #602 "*It's Not Just a Theory*" for a study of this process.]

It is not God's will that any man be in the condition of demonic possession. But demonic possession can be the *secondary* result of man willfully disobeying God's will.

Thus it is the violation of God's will *by* man; which then results in a condition that is not God's will *for* man. In the case of Job, this was permission for the enemy to *attack*, (but not possess or kill), Job. In the case of possession; although the magnitudes may be different; the balancing *process* is nevertheless quite similar.

So *if* there is a verse 21, or perhaps better stated if verse 21 is an actuality; it seems that there are then *two* ways presented to cast out a demon.

One is *direct* and based upon the force created both by the will and the faith or belief of man, consistent with that which Jesus spoke in verse 20.

The other, is the creation of an immaterial imbalance by praying and fasting. This would represent an *indirect* action; as this force is not "directly directed" at the demon, which is the purported reason for verse 21.

What the question here *is not*; is whether the creation of a sufficient immaterial imbalance can sometimes provide God with sufficient "license" to cast out a demon, as this can happen.

Why license? Because if license were not required, and possession is against God's will; why then does He not just do it Himself without any "prayer and fasting?"

The answer is that He cannot do this without simultaneously *violating* His own laws. Man had previously been given this authority in Genesis 1:28. Thus for God to do this directly *Himself*, an immaterial imbalance created by man's will in prayer and fasting is required, in order to "pay" for;" i.e.; *balance*; this action on the part of God.

What the question here actually *is*; is whether or not Jesus made this statement in response to the inquiry as to why the disciples failed. The clear and convincing evidence is that He did not.

Thus with verse 21 removed, it was not the absence of prayer and fasting that caused, or even had anything to do with this failure of the disciples attempts. But rather, it was insufficient *faith*—just as Jesus stated in the verse, (verse 20), immediately preceding verse 21.

In order to maintain intellectual honesty, it must be noted that when what appears to be this same story appears in Mark, words similar to the "phantom" verse of Mathew 17:21 are included.

Mark 9:18-22 (KJV) tells us:

> *"And wheresoever he taketh him,*
> *he teareth him: and he foameth,*
> *and gnasheth with his teeth,*
> *and pineth away: and I spake to*
> *thy disciples that they should cast him out;*
> *and they could not.*
> *He answereth him, and saith,*
> *O faithless generation,*
> *how long shall I be with you?*
> *how long shall I suffer you?*
> *bring him unto me.*
>
> *And they brought him unto him:*
> *and when he saw him,*
> *straightway the spirit tare him;*
> *and he fell on the ground,*
> *and wallowed foaming.*
>
> *And he asked his father,*
> *How long is it ago since this*
> *came unto him?*
> *And he said, Of a child.*
> *And ofttimes it hath cast him into the fire,*
> *and into the waters, to destroy him:*
> *but if thou canst do any thing,*
> *have compassion on us, and help us."*[28]

Here in Mark, is a description of the condition of the boy. It is interesting that in the beginning of these passages, the demon is referred to as "he" and "him;" but in the last passage is referred to as "it."

The father is telling Jesus, that Jesus' disciples could not cast "him" out. Here he is not asking Jesus *why* the disciples failed, but rather is asking Jesus for help: "*if thou canst do any thing, have compassion on us, and help us.*"

Mark 9:23-29 continues the *story*:

"Jesus said unto him, If thou canst believe, all things are possible to him that believeth.

And straightway the father of the child cried out, and said with tears,

Lord, I believe; help thou mine unbelief. When Jesus saw that the people came running together, he rebuked the foul spirit, saying unto him, Thou dumb and deaf spirit, I charge thee, come out of him, and enter no more into him.

And the spirit cried, and rent him sore, and came out of him: and he was as one dead; insomuch that many said, He is dead. But Jesus took him by the hand, and lifted him up; and he arose.

And when he was come into the house, his disciples asked him privately, Why could not we cast him out? And he said unto them,

INEVITABLE BALANCE

This kind can come forth by nothing, but by prayer and fasting."[29]

At the end, is the verse similar to the "phantom" verse Matthew 17:21, but appears here in Mark 9:29: "*And he said unto them, This kind can come forth by nothing, but by prayer and fasting.*"

The actual Greek word translated as "nothing" is:

> "3762 ŏuděis,; include. fem. ŏuděmia,; and neut. ŏuděn,; from 3761 and 1520; *not even one* (man woman or thing), i.e. *none, nobody, nothing...*"[30]

The use of *ŏuděis* here by Mark is quite inclusive or exclusive depending upon ones perspective: "Not even one man woman or thing."

So here it seems like: "This kind can come forth by *not even one man woman or thing*, but (only) by prayer and fasting." There seems to be disagreement as to whether the word "fasting" is actually present, but this matters little.

Thus according to *Mark*, while in *public*, Jesus seems to be telling the *father* of the boy, ("Jesus said unto *him*"); that all things are possible to those who believe or have faith: "*If thou canst believe, all things are possible to him that believeth.*"

The question is whether Jesus was answering here the *yet unasked* question as to why it was that the disciples failed, (as later asked Him by the *disciples* in

Matthew); or if Jesus was explaining to the boy's' father why he, (the father), himself was unable to do it?

One could argue that Jesus' statement had nothing to do with either; but rather was linking *Jesus'* own ability to cast it out to level of the man's' belief or faith. But if thought through, contextually the latter would seem to make little or no sense.

We do know how this message was received by the father, because he immediately, (straightway or straightaway). responded: *"And straightway the father of the child cried out, and said with tears, Lord, I believe; help thou mine unbelief."*

Thus the father is led to believe that this was referring to the father's unbelief, and not that of the disciples.

But then here when in *private*, Jesus; unlike in Matthew; says nothing about the level of His disciples' or anyone else's *belief* or *faith*.

Instead, He only tells his disciples that what He had just told the father in public does not in any way apply here, as ŏudĕis, or "not even one man woman or thing" is sufficient; but only by prayer, and possibly also fasting, this *"kind can come forth,"* or out.

According to *Matthew*, when in *public*, Jesus seems to "answer" the man—at least about *something*, stating: *"O faithless and perverse generation, how long shall I be with you? how long shall I suffer you? bring him hither to me."*

There is no *public* mention in Matthew of belief or faith—no mustard seeds or mountains when in *public*. And obviously, in no way do the disciples consider this as any answer as to why they failed prior to the appearance of the word "*apart*."

And also according to Matthew, then when in *private* ("apart"), Jesus tells his *disciples "Why could not we cast him out?"* is *"Because of your unbelief; for verily I say unto you, If ye have faith as a grain of mustard seed, ye shall say unto this mountain, Remove hence to yonder place; and it shall remove; and nothing shall be impossible unto you,"* just prior to the appearance of the "phantom" verse 21.

Thus if Mark 9 verse 29 is to be considered as genuine; it must be asked why Jesus would state that "*all*;" again a rather inclusive term; things are possible: "If thou canst believe, all things are possible to him that believeth." when in public? And then subsequently when in private, with respect to the very same matter; state with equal inclusivity or exclusivity that *ŏudĕis* or "*Not even one man woman or thing*;" could do this?

The likely answer, is that He could not and did not. In addition, if Jesus as a *man* is included in *ŏudĕis*, He would arguably be stating that He alone could not do what He did. Thus verse 29 seems to be merely a recapitulation of this "phantom" verse contained in Matthew.

What is insufficient faith? Is this in actuality the *absence* of a sufficient quantity of faith; or can this better be understood as the *presence* of some degree of doubt?

Jesus also told us that faith in the quantity of a mustard seed had the power to move a mountain; so how much faith would then be required to cast out a demon; that is *required* to obey the will of man?

If it is stipulated that verse 21 in Matthew, and verse 29 in Mark, (hereafter collectively referred to as verse 21), were added; it then must be asked why?

The true answer, is that verse 21 was added to cause *reasonable doubt*. (*Present* tense is used here deliberately, as it still can and does.) If verse 20 is understood, and verse 21 were unknown; then any doubt in man's ability to cast out demons; either because he ate lunch that day, or forgot to pray that day, would be *unreasonable*. This would also be the case regarding any reasonable doubt because of the *length* of any fast, or the *amount* of any prayer. In fact, this would not even be considered.

But by adding verse 21, things become unclear, and thus would cause reasonable doubt and questioning: "Is this one of those demons to which verse 20 refers; or is it one of those demons to which verse 21 refers?"

In the end, because of this *doubt*, (insufficient faith), all demons then by *design* will ultimately become those that verse 21 falsely refers to; as demons will exploit this doubt, just as was done here in Matthew. "Did I pray long enough?" "Did I fast long enough?"

It is the intention of verse 21 to change a binary to an analog. This easily can create more than enough "reasonable doubt" to cause failure.

In the sixty-six books that comprise the standard Bible, it is staggering as to how few actual *informative* references there are to the enemy. The reason for this is simple. Utilizing those whom he could control, the enemy simply had these references removed long long ago. This was phase *one*.

Phase *two*, was the mistranslations, today known colloquially as Bible "versions."

And phase *three* was the addition of verses such as Matthew 17:21 and Mark 9:29. With regard to Matthew 17:21, KJV "bought it," NAS straddled the issue, and NIV simply discarded it.

The enemy has, and has always had two serious problems:

The *first* is the matter of the previously referenced *hierarchy*. As a matter of *authority*, the enemy must in the general sense obey the will of man.

And more specifically; to the extent that the enemy is acting *against* the will of God, the enemy must obey man's will when man's will is consistent with God's will; e.g.; removal of demonic *possession*.

This hierarchy or authority matter, has essentially been a constant since early Genesis. And because of Calvary, the "power equation" shifted substantially in man's favor.

This is a *binary* with regard to casting out a demon.

The enemy is in a constant war with man in order to affect said (man's) *will*. In this usage, "will" is not merely wishing or hoping. "Where there is a will, there is a way;" is often heard. Another version is: "Where there is a will, there are relatives." Although the latter is provided as humor; nevertheless; whenever man wishes to act in a manner consistent with God's will, in certain senses, each is are true.

Will in furtherance of God's will often provide a "way," including *dunamis* or supernatural power—just as Jesus tells us.

And this "will" also attracts those who want to at a minimum to dissipate this will. These particular "relatives," are the "one third" we are *not* told went with him. Like moths drawn to a light source, they come to provide interference. Although it is beyond the scope of this Monograph, when it is the case that this light source is actually a *flame*; the results can become a bit interesting.

When *expressed*, as previously stated; *will* represents a force in the immaterial realm. When there is "doubt in will," this then arguably represents an oxymoronic expression.

As long as there is doubt, or perhaps better stated to the extent there is doubt; there is not will. Casting out a demon while *hoping* he will leave, is not an expression of will, but merely expressing desire. It is in furtherance of this conversion of *will* to mere *desire*, that is the main purpose for the creation and inclusion of these, as well as other, "phantom verses."

The *second* problem the enemy has; is one that has become substantially worse for him since Calvary. This second problem is that which Jesus referenced back in John 14:12—most particularly the *"greater works than these shall he do"* part.

And the enemy also knows very well the qualification, or the *"believeth"* part. Only Jesus is *The* Anointed One, and the enemy did not fare very well with Him. But anyone can be *An* Anointed one, with powers *greater* than those of The Anointed One—at least according to He Who was The Anointed One.

INEVITABLE BALANCE

Thus in keeping with KJV style, it *"behooveth"* the enemy to attack said *"believeth."* This gives the enemy two distinct advantages:

The *first*, is to prevent man from having the *knowledge* of man's true capabilities.

And the *second*, is to see to it that man does not *qualify* for any *greater* capabilities.

Today's war on *Christianity* is therefore actually an attack on Jesus; or the *second* part of the Trinity, largely in an *indirect* manner. The enemy fears Jesus for certain; but what he is *terrified* of, is the utilization of the *Christos*, or anointing of the *third* part of the Trinity upon man.

Jesus provision of *justification* or *salvation* for the immaterial portion of man, was a part of a larger redemptive process at; and just prior to; Calvary. [See Monograph: *"Calvary's Hidden Truths"*]

Whether or not one chooses to *believe* that this is true, in no way changes that which is *purported* to be. Salvation/justification is an important part of, but only a part of, what we are told Jesus provided; and non-believers cannot in any way alter this. One is free to not believe it; however unbelief in this, is an insufficient means or justification for any changes in what is or is not stated.

But as stated in John 14:12, Jesus also ultimately provided additional miraculous capabilities, (dunamis), which are even greater than His had been. The enemy's knowledge and fear of man's increase in available *dunamis*, or supernatural power; whether *consciously* known by the anti-Christians or not; represents the main reason behind today's war on Christianity.

Tacit knowledge is knowledge that one "knows;" but one does not know he knows. This is "not knowing, (not being consciously aware of), what one *knows*;" as opposed to: "not knowing what one *does not know*."

"Christians" are of course free to espouse *realities* that make little or no sense, and thus these cannot possibly be true.

Proselytizing that a man that we are told was *formed* from *something*; not only *could* be, but in fact *is* the very same man that we are previously told was brought into existence from *nothing*; simply makes no degree of sense. And there is a price tag for this; "including but not limited to;" the ultimate result of prospective "believers" who must then discard science in order to become a believer—and many will simply discard these erroneous representations of the Bible and Christianity instead.

Likewise; it must be asked how is it that three days and three nights "like Jonah;" can somehow be "squeezed in" from Friday 3:00 PM until before early dawn on Sunday?

"This one" is the result of simply misunderstanding, through ignorance or otherwise; as to which particular "Sabbath" it is to which the Bible refers.

Willful proffering realities such as these; i.e.; at best "misinformation;" not only affects those who currently believe in Christianity, but also as stated: *prospective* Christians. This pleases the enemy greatly; but has nothing to do with what the Bible tells us—if the same is merely read without prejudice. Thus none of this has any effects whatsoever on the *actualities* involved.

INEVITABLE BALANCE

The enemy was there, and he knows what exists; and thus he acts from a *reality* in accordance with these *actualities*—at least to the extent that he is able. It is true that "the truth is not in him." But this does not necessarily mean that he would touch a red-hot stove repeatedly.

It is extremely important to recognize that there is no such thing as a stimulus without a response. Neither is there any such thing as a response without a stimulus. The only known exception to this rule is God. It is God, and God alone that has or had no cause. He is the *primum movens*, or prime mover.

It is also important to recognize that there are two realms. One by definition contains matter and is referred to as the *material* realm. The other contains no matter and is referred to as the *immaterial* realm. This distinction is a binary.

The cause for the effect known as the material realm could not have existed in a yet to be created material realm. Thus the cause for this effect had to have been in the *immaterial* realm prior to the creation of this material realm. Science refers to the creation of the material realm as the "Big Bang;" with the very same event being described in Genesis 1:1.

Things that reside solely in the material realm, only affect the material realm. But anything that is dual in nature; i.e.; contains the "breath of life;" is a dual being. The actions of any dual being affect both realms.

In a sense it is like two "closed" systems with a portal between the two. In an absolute sense, one cannot light a match and not create an imbalance by increasing the temperature of the earth—however miniscule this change might be. And this very same action produces an imbalance in the immaterial realm depending on the *reasons* for the action.

All dual fold actions, (*action* and *reason*), are subject to similar laws; with balancing mechanisms for each.

Again assuming that any "key to the universe" actually exists, it could be argued from a very broad perspective that understanding *will* and *balance* represents this key.

When H. Sapiens exercise free will in the performance of any action or inaction; (Yup, that one sometimes counts too.); the results are not limited to the *reality* of the actions, but rather are determined by the *actuality* of the action.

From the standpoint of universal law, whatever one chooses to do to another; it is simultaneously chosen by him or her that the very same be done to them. It *is* one in the same—an indivisible package. Human realities can try to separate this actuality into a reality that suits them at the time, but this merely represents delusion.

When one gives, an actuality is created that requires giving back to the giver. But the calculations include the *reasons*. This is what Jesus was trying to teach people. And when one steals, an actuality is created that requires taking from the thief. Thus the "do unto others" admonition represents solid advice—for these very reasons.

Choose actions carefully, and choose *motives* even more carefully; as they will be balanced—*always*. It may look good or bad for a while, depending on the nature of the action; but the balance is inevitable.

ABOUT THE MEEKRAKER SERIES

What on earth is a MeekRaker?
This word can be broken down into two parts "Meek" and "Raker." Capital letters were used in order to minimize any mispronunciations such as Mee-kraker; but the "etymology" is actually the fusion of these two words.

What is meek? And who in their right mind would ever want to be meek? Courage, strength, and bravery are characteristics that are generally considered desirable; but meek? No thanks. Unfortunately, the meaning of this word has been distorted over time to include things such as timidity, or shyness; weakness, or cowardice, but this is not; or rather should not be so.

Chambers states:

> "meek adj. Probably before 1200 meok gentle, humble, in Ancrene Riwle; later mec (probably about 1200, in the *The Ormlum*);

borrowed from a Scandanavian source (Compare Old Icelandic mjukr soft pliant gentle...."[AT-1]

These origins seem to be adjectival in nature, and describe a condition of humility or softness. Thus a meek person, by these definitions would indicate a humble or soft person. The opposite of this would then be a person who is prideful or hard.

Humble vs. prideful is an easy one. Who would want to be prideful? The Bible is replete with warnings about pride; and it was pride that started all of the messes to begin with. Pride may make one "feel good" for a short period of time, but as previously referenced; the Bible is quite clear that on that path there lies destruction.

But what does the Bible actually have to say about being a meek person?

- It tells us that the meek shall (*not will or might*) inherit the earth.[AT-2]
- It further tells us that the meek will be guided in judgment will be taught His way.[AT-3]
- The meek will be lifted up by the Lord, and He will cast the wicked down to the ground.[AT-4]
- He will save all the meek of the earth.[AT-5]

And what about the Bible's statements regarding being "hard?"

- "For their heart was hardened."[AT-6] "Have ye your heart yet hardened?"[AT-7]
- "... their eyes and hardened their heart."[AT-8]
- "But they and our fathers dealt proudly, and hardened their necks, and hearkened not to thy commandments, and refused to obey, neither were mindful of thy wonders that thou didst among them; but hardened their necks, and in their rebellion..."[AT-9]
- "Happy is the man that feareth always: But he that hardeneth his heart shall fall into mischief."[AT-10]
- "He that being often reproved hardeneth his neck, shall suddenly be destroyed, and that without remedy."[AT-11]

The actual word in all of these citations which is translated as hard is:

> "4456 poroo (a kind of stone); to *petrify*, i.e. (fig.) to *indurate* (*render stupid* or *callous*): - blind, harden.[AT-12]

With respect to hard, there is a clear Scriptural relationship between the same and disobedience; not being "mindful" of God performing wonders in one's life, rebellious, falling into "mischief," and being "destroyed," "without remedy."

In addition, by the very definition of the original word, one who is "hard" is also stupid callous and blind. (If a physical heart were actually to turn into stone, you are just dead; so surely that definition does not apply in this context or usage.)

Thus, meek or soft; that being the opposite of hard; would tend to be obedient, be mindful of God performing wonders, not rebellious, not falling into mischief, and not destroyed. Furthermore, one would not be "stupid," "callous" or "blind."

The use of the term meek as "soft," also implies *teachable*.

Hardhead: will not change mind. Hardhearted: will not change heart. Hard necked: junction between head and heart is hard, and will not permit mental change to be transmitted to change the heart.

If it is firmly established that the term "revelation" has the prerequisite of being *the* truth; when confronted with potential revelation; it has been the authors' experiences that hard persons; specifically those of the head, neck, and heart variety; will generally behave according to the "Three A's:"

> A_1 is *anger*. This is the first response. This anger is not so much because there is a remote chance that they may be wrong, but rather when it is somewhat clear that they *are* wrong. This would be best illustrated as a line on a graph rising from left to right; with the level of anger represented by the vertical axis, and time represented by the horizontal axis.
>
> A_2 is *argument*. This generally begins with emotionally (anger) driven arguments. As

the arguments begin to fail, the level and usually the slope of A_1 will increase. When all possible arguments, logical, relevant or otherwise have been proffered, the original arguments will then return. This would be best illustrated as a circle under the rising anger line referenced above. Often, what is just under the skin, (which is generally the reason for the pride and subsequent anger) will pop its "head" out; revealing things previously unknown about this individual.

A_3 is *absconding*. When all of the arguments and the repetition thereof have unquestionably failed, the hard person will generally abscond; or run away. This may be represented by actual physical separation, changing the subject or in some other manner. This could be perceived as the disappearance of the anger line, but is only subjective; as the true level of anger then becomes somewhat hidden.

Contrarily, the *meek* will weigh the value of any purported revelation; and then decide precisely what it is that merits their belief. Sincere questioning and even some arguments will be presented; but here not with the primary purpose of proving that they, the inquirer, is correct; but rather to understand precisely what it is that this revelation represents; knowing that if it in fact does represent revelation, then this will be to their benefit. A logical decision will then be made with respect to what constitutes the truth.

The primary basis for the actions of a "hard-head," is *emotional*. The primary basis for the actions of the meek; although perhaps including some emotional factors; (i.e. passion); is largely *intellectual*.

In a sense, the purpose of a rake is to separate the soft from the hard. The Bible refers to separating the wheat from the chaff, the silver from the dross; hence the origin of "*MeekRaker*". Meek or hard is not so much determined by what one believes; but rather by the *process* involved in making these determinations.

Bibliography

1. *Chambers Dictionary of Etymology*. Copyright © 1988 The H. W. Wilson Company, New York, NY p. 72
2. *New American Standard Bible*: 1995 update. 1995 (Genesis 1:1) The Lockman Foundation: Lahabra, CA
3. *King James Bible* Matthew 19:26
4. *King James Bible* John 14:12
5. Strong, James. *Strong's Exhaustive Concordance of the Bible*. © 1890 James Strong, Madison, NJ p. 49 (Greek)
6. Quadrakoff, Emma, *The Emmanic Principles* © 2017 Quadrakoff Publications Group, LLC Wilmington Delaware
7. *King James Bible* Genesis 2:7
8. Quadrakoff, Emma, *The Emmanic Principles* © 2017 Quadrakoff Publications Group, LLC Wilmington Delaware
9. *New American Standard Bible*: 1995 update. 1995 (Malachi 3:10) The Lockman Foundation: Lahabra, CA
10. Strong, James. *Strong's Exhaustive Concordance of the Bible*. © 1890 James Strong, Madison, NJ p. 817 (Hebrew)
11. *Physicsclassroom.com*

12. *New American Standard Bible*: 1995 update. 1995 (Proverbs 16:2) The Lockman Foundation: Lahabra, CA
13. *Physicsclassroom.com*
14. *Physicsclassroom.com*
15. *New American Standard Bible*: 1995 update. 1995 (2 Corinthians 9:7) The Lockman Foundation: Lahabra, CA
16. *King James Bible* John 14:12
17. *King James Bible* Matthew 17:14-19
18. *King James Bible* Matthew 17:20
19. *King James Bible* Matthew 17:21
20. *King James Bible* Matthew 17:22
21. *New American Standard Bible*: 1995 update. 1995 (Matthew 17:20) The Lockman Foundation: Lahabra, CA
22. *New American Standard Bible*: 1995 update. 1995 (2 Matthew 17:21) The Lockman Foundation: Lahabra, CA
23. *New American Standard Bible*: 1995 update. 1995 (Matthew 17:22) The Lockman Foundation: Lahabra, CA
24. *New American Standard Bible*: 1995 update. 1995 The Lockman Foundation: Lahabra, CA introductory pages, not numbered
25. *The Holy Bible New International Version* © 1973, 1978, 1984 International Bible Society (Matthew 17: 20)
26. *The Holy Bible New International Version* © 1973, 1978, 1984 International Bible Society (Matthew 17: 21)
27. *The Holy Bible New International Version* © 1973, 1978, 1984 International Bible Society (Matthew 17: 22)
28. *King James Bible* Mark 9:18-22
29. *King James Bible* Mark 9:23-29

Bibliography

30. Strong, James. *Strong's Exhaustive Concordance of the Bible.* © 1890 James Strong, Madison, NJ p. 53 (Greek)

About the MeekRaker Series

AT1 *Chambers Dictionary of Etymology.* Copyright © 1988 The H. W. Wilson Company, New York, NY p.648

AT2 *www.kingjamesbibleonline.org* (KJV) (Matt.5:5) retrieved June 2011

AT3 *www.kingjamesbibleonline.org* (KJV) (Ps. 25:9) retrieved June 2011

AT4 *www.kingjamesbibleonline.org* (KJV) (Ps. 147:6) retrieved June 2011

AT5 *www.kingjamesbibleonline.org* (KJV) (Ps. 76:9) retrieved June 2011

AT6 *www.kingjamesbibleonline.org* (KJV) (Mark 6:52) retrieved June 2011

AT7 *www.kingjamesbibleonline.org* (KJV) (Mark 8:17) retrieved June 2011

AT8 *www.kingjamesbibleonline.org* (KJV) (John 12:40) retrieved June 2011

AT9 *www.kingjamesbibleonline.org* (KJV) (Neh. 9:16)
    retrieved June 2011
AT10 *www.kingjamesbibleonline.org* (KJV) (Prov. 28:14)
    retrieved June 2011
AT11 *www.kingjamesbibleonline.org* (KJV) (Prov. 29:1)
    retrieved June 2011
AT12 Strong, James. *Strong's Exhaustive Concordance of the Bible.* © 1890 James Strong, Madison, NJ p. 63 (Greek)

Other Fine QPG Publications:

MeekRaker Beginnings...

From the inside flap of *"MeekRaker Beginnings..."*

"The primary purpose of this tome, is the reconciliation of the word of God with science; and to do so in such a manner as to be rendered inarguable by any rational mind. As stated in the Preface: "One must choose between being a "man of science" or a believer," because they are generally considered to be mutually exclusive. If one agrees that words mean things, then an unbiased fair read of God's Word presents no such paradox. But one must read what God actually said, not merely what one thinks He said, what one was told He said, what one wished He said, or would rather He had said."

Wisdom Essentials—*The Pentalogy*

"That Which is Difficult If Not Impossible to Find Anywhere Else—All In One Volume."

But there are many other effects for which no material cause can be found. In *"Donald Trump*

Candidacy According to Matthew?," his meteoric rise and seeming inability to fail are explained according to Biblical principles. Since this is a non-political work, his success was not actually prophesied, but no other conclusion could possibly have been drawn—*and this was published long before he was even nominated.*

In *"SHÂMAR TO SHARIA,"* the process of radical indoctrination is analyzed, and is shown to be a perversion of that very same thing God instructed man to do with the Commandments, and how this is not in any way limited to terrorists.

"It's Not Just A Theory" examines the relationship between behavior and longevity according to both science and the Scriptures; and "according to both" also includes major consistencies.

"Calvary's Hidden Truths" reveals many unknown facts about what actually occurred at that time.

"Inevitable Balance" scientifically and Biblically explains that which is often observed but rarely understood: Why "What Goes Around Comes Around;" AKA *karma*, or the "law of compensation."

STATISTS SAVING ONE

"The Malignant Sophistry of Rights Removal by the Far Left"

"...under the umbrella of "liberals" or "liberalism;" (as used today); there are actually two separate and distinct groups:

"True liberals believe very much in what they promulgate. They are truly concerned with the welfare of citizens, and they believe in policies that will benefit the same—at least in their view. There are neither nefarious purposes, nor any intellectual dishonesty. Their objective is to improve the quality of life (and longevity), for as many people as possible.

"...Conservatives and liberals can often agree on the ends; but vastly disagree on the means. Giving a hungry person a fish is kind; but to conservatives, teaching him how to fish seems to be a better long term solution. It is not that conservatives object to the temporary giving of the fish; but rather they object to not teaching him how to fish.

"True liberals believe in the dignity of man; and promulgate policies in furtherance of this belief.
"Statists; the other group usually and often erroneously grouped under the "liberal" umbrella; are another matter. It is because of agreements with liberal policy that they are usually grouped under this liberal umbrella;

but their motivations, purposes and beliefs are entirely different—arguably antithetical—to true liberalism."

OSTIUM AB INFERNO
[*The Opening From Hell*]

"The Original Monograph - According to the Father, The Christ Son and The Holy Ghost"

"What is hell?
Why is there a hell?
What openings from "hell" exist?
What is the truth about "Abraham's Bosom?" And how does this or do these affect man?
What are angels? Are angels named such because of structure or function? Precisely why were some angels sent to hell? Is it true that one third were banished to hell? And when did this all happen?
Much of that which is fanciful has been written about these questions. But the answers should not be sought from that which is the product of men's imaginations—albeit these may provide interesting reading. Rather; the answers should be sought from, and always remain: "according to The Father, The Christ Son, and The Holy Ghost." (Written in English.)

REINCARNATION —A REASONABLE INQUIRY

"Often times it is emotion(s) and not facts that determine what it is that is believed to be 'in fact so.'" —p.6

"When truth and perceived practicality conflict; unfortunately it is truth that often becomes the sacrificial lamb." —p.91

"He that answereth a matter before he heareth it, it is folly and shame unto him."
                              —Proverbs 18:13 (KJV)

Some say reincarnation is a fact, and cite the Bible as the unimpeachable source regarding this matter.

Others say reincarnation is fiction, and cite the Bible as the unimpeachable source regarding this very same matter.

One of these groups is about to be shocked.

QPG Publications are available
wherever you buy fine books.

For a full list of QPG publications,
visit us at MeekRaker.com